Papatango Theatre Con

The world premiere of tl
2017 Papatango New W

CW00347021

TRESTLE

by Stewart Pringle

First performance at Southwark Playhouse, London:
Wednesday 1 November 2017

TRESTLE

by Stewart Pringle

Cast in order of speaking

Harry	**Gary Lilburn**
Denise	**Connie Walker**

Director	**Cathal Cleary**
Designer	**Frankie Bradshaw**
Lighting Designer	**Johanna Town**
Music and Sound Designer	**Richard Hammarton**
Producer	**Chris Foxon**
Dramaturg	**George Turvey**
Production Manager	**Ian Taylor for eStage Production**
Stage Manager	**Edwina Allen**

Cast and Creative Team

Gary Lilburn | Harry

Theatre includes *The Taming of the Shrew, A Midsummer Night's Dream* and *The Golden Ass* (Shakespeare's Globe); *All That Fall* (Out of Joint); *Deluge, Buried Alive* and *Tuesday's Child* (Hampstead Theatre); *The Cripple of Inishmann* (West End/Broadway); *Dr Faustus* (West Yorkshire Playhouse/Glasgow Citizens); *The Kingdom* and *Angels and Saints* (Soho Theatre); *The Hairy Ape* and *The Hostage* (Southwark Playhouse); *Buried Child* (The Curve, Leicester); *16 Possible Glimpses* (Abbey Theatre); *Loot* (Hull Truck); *Calendar Girls* (Chichester/West End); *The Man Who Had All The Luck* (Donmar Warehouse); *Living Quarters* (Edinburgh Lyceum); *Dancing at Lughnasa* (Manchester Library Theatre); *The Quare Fellow* (Tricycle Theatre/Oxford Stage Company); *To Kill a Mockingbird, Death of a Salesman* and *Dolly West's Kitchen* (Leicester Haymarket); *Hen House* (Arcola Theatre); *The Weir* (Royal Court Theatre); *The Measles* (Gate Theatre); *Rhinoceros* (Riverside Studios) and *Desire Under the Elms* (Shared Experience).

Film includes *Philomena, Eden, Garage,* and *Veronica Guerin.*

Television includes *Paula, Catastrophe, Doctors, Mrs Brown's Boys, Dead or Alive, Pete Versus Life, I Shouldn't Be Alive, Casualty, The Bill, Whistleblower, Single Handed, Perfect Day the Funeral, Pulling, Sea of Souls, Grease Monkeys II, 55° North, The Good Thief, EastEnders, Dalziel and Pascoe, McCready & Daughter, My Family, Fair City, A Safe House, Perfect Scoundrels* and *Single in London.*

Radio includes *What Will Survive, All That Fall, Love in Recovery* and *Lady Audley's Secret.*

Connie Walker | Denise

Theatre includes *The March on Russia* (Orange Tree Theatre); *Death of a Salesman* (Northampton/UK tour); *A Month of Sundays* (Queens Theatre Hornchurch); *Folk* (Birmingham Rep/tour); *Seeing the Lights, Kes* and *Top Girls* (New Vic Theatre); *To Kill a Mockingbird* (Regent's Park Open Air Theatre/UK tour/Barbican); *An Inspector Calls* and *Death Trap* (English Theatre Frankfurt); *As You Like It* and *Hayfever* (West Yorkshire Playhouse); *The Beauty Queen of Leenane* (London Classics Theatre UK & Ireland tour); *Separate Tables* (Chichester Festival Theatre); *Spring Awakening* (Novello Theatre); *Plunder* (Watermill Theatre/Greenwich Theatre); *Inside Out* (Arcola Theatre/UK tour); *Happy Birthday Brecht* (National Theatre); *Mother Courage* (Ipswich Wolsey Theatre) and *Much Ado About Nothing* (Manchester Royal Exchange).

Film includes *What Do You See?* and *The Darkest Light.*

Television includes *Holby City, Coronation Street, Vera, Scott & Bailey, Hollyoaks, Doctors, Silent Witness, Casualty, Secret Diary of a Call Girl, New Tricks, Blackpool, M.I.T., The Vice* and *The Bill.*

Radio includes *The Chausseur and the Nun, Stage Fright* and *Antony and Cleopatra.*

Stewart Pringle | Playwright

Stewart's recent work for stage includes *The Ghost Hunter* and *You Look Tasty!*. He is currently the Associate Dramaturg of the Bush Theatre, and prior to that was Artistic Director of the Old Red Lion Theatre in Islington, for which he received the 2016 Off West End Award for Best Artistic Director. In 2011 he co-founded the London Horror Festival, now in its seventh year. Working as a theatre critic for several years, his writing has been published in *The Stage*, *Time Out*, *New Scientist* and *Exeunt Magazine*.

Cathal Cleary | Director

Cathal is the Artistic Director of MOMMO Theatre and was the first Trainee Artistic Director at the Donmar Warehouse from 2014–2016. He won the 2011 JMK Award.

Theatre as director includes *The Half of It* (Dublin Fringe, First Fortnight Award); *Furniture* (Druid Debuts); *Disco Pigs* (Young Vic, JMK Award/UK & Irish tour); *Women of Troy* (Mountview); *The Last Yankee* (Print Room); *Appointment in Limbo* (Dublin Fringe) and *The Factory Girls* and *The Cripple of Inishmaan* (Town Hall Galway).

Theatre as associate director includes *The Vote* (Donmar/More4).

Theatre as assistant director includes *The Winslow Boy* (Old Vic); *Privates on Parade* (MGC); *Timon of Athens* and *Detroit* (National Theatre); *Twisted Tales* (Lyric Hammersmith) and *The Beauty Queen of Leenane* (Young Vic).

Frankie Bradshaw | Designer

Theatre as designer includes *Orca* (Papatango at Southwark Playhouse); *Adding Machine* (Finborough Theatre; winner of the 2016 Off West End Award for Best Set Design); *Private Lives* (London Classic Theatre UK tour); *Di and Viv and Rose* (Stephen Joseph Theatre); *Nesting* (Watermill Theatre); *Assata Taught Me* (Gate Theatre); *Moth* (Hope Mill Theatre); *Clickbait* and *A First World Problem* (Theatre503); *Barbarians* (Young Vic; JMK Award 2015, Olivier Award nominated); *Grav* (Torch Theatre, Wales); *Stories from the Sea* (Unity Theatre, Liverpool); *Punk Rock* (Actor's Studio, Liverpool) and *A Picture of Dorian Gray* and *The Comedy of Errors* (LIPA, Liverpool).

Site-specific work includes co-designing *Karagula* (STYX, Tottenham) and *If Walls Could Talk: 100 Seel Street* (Seel Street, Liverpool). Frankie has also designed the Young Vic's *5 Plays 5 Days* and *Fresh Direction* projects and has worked as associate designer to Christopher Oram on many productions including *The Winter's Tale, Harlequinade, Romeo and Juliet* and *The Entertainer* (Garrick Theatre); *Man and Superman* (National Theatre); *Photograph 51* (Noël Coward Theatre); *Hughie* (Booth Theatre, New York) and *Damsel in Distress* (Chichester Festival Theatre).

Frankie was a Linbury Prize finalist in 2015, working with the Lyric Theatre, Belfast.

www.frankiebradshawdesign.com

Johanna Town | Lighting Designer

Johanna has designed the lighting for numerous major theatre and opera companies both in the UK and internationally, including: The National Theatre, RSC, West Yorkshire Playhouse, Sheffield Theatres, Royal Exchange Theatre, Manchester, and Chichester Festival Theatre, to name but a few, as well as productions in the West End, on Broadway, and abroad. She has designed over fifty productions for the Royal Court Theatre in London where she was Head of Lighting for seventeen years.

Her most recent productions include *Fracked!* (Jonathan Church productions); *Julius Caesar* (Sheffield Theatres); *Miss Julie* and *Remarkable Invisible* (Theatre by the Lake); *Fox on the Fairway* (Queens Theatre); *The Norman Conquests* (Chichester Festival Theatre); *The Cherry Orchard* (Guildhall School of Music and Drama) and *Guys & Dolls* (Royal Exchange Theatre, Manchester).

Johanna is an Associate Artist for Theatre503, as well as the Professional Rep for the Association of Lighting Designers where she has a regular column in Focus magazine. She was made a Fellow of Guildhall School of Music and Drama for her contribution to lighting design in theatre.

This is Johanna's third production for Papatango following *Tomcat* and *Orca* (2015 and 2016 Papatango New Writing Prize winners, both at Southwark Playhouse).

Richard Hammarton | Music and Sound Designer

Theatre includes *Orca* and *Tomcat* (Papatango at Southwark Playhouse); *After Independence* (Papatango at Arcola Theatre); *The Weir* (English Touring Theatre); *Girls* (HighTide Festival Theatre/Soho Theatre); *Burning Doors* (Belarus Free Theatre); *Much Ado About Nothing* and *Jumpy* (Theatr Clwyd); *Linda* (Royal Court Theatre); *The Crucible, Brilliant Adventures, Edward II* and *Dr Faustus* (Royal Exchange Theatre, Manchester); *A Number* (Nuffield Theatre/Young Vic); *Crushed Shells and Mud* (Southwark Playhouse); *Comrade Fiasco* (Gate Theatre); *Grimm Tales 2* (Bargehouse, Oxo Tower Wharf); *Beached* (Marlowe Theatre/Soho Theatre); *The Pitchfork Disney* and *Ghost from a Perfect Place* (Arcola Theatre); *The Crucible* (Old Vic); *Dealer's Choice* (Royal & Derngate Theatre); *Kingston 14* (Theatre Royal Stratford East); *Sunspots, Deposit* and *Fault Lines* (Hampstead Theatre); *Early Days (of a Better Nation)* (Battersea Arts Centre); *Sizwe Bansi is Dead* and *Six Characters Looking for an Author* (Young Vic); *The Taming of the Shrew* (Shakespeare's Globe); *Speaking in Tongues* (Duke of York's Theatre); *A Raisin in the Sun* (Lyric Hammersmith/national tour); *The Last Summer* (Gate Theatre, Dublin); *Mudlarks* (HighTide Festiva/Theatre503/Bush Theatre); *Ghosts* (Duchess Theatre); *Judgement Day* (Print Room); *Persuasion, The Constant Wife, Les Liaisons Dangereuses, Arsenic and Old Lace, The Real Thing* and *People at Sea* (Salisbury Playhouse); *Platform* (Old Vic Tunnels); *Pride and Prejudice* (Theatre Royal Bath/national tour); *Dealer's Choice* (Birmingham Rep); *Hello and Goodbye* and *Some Kind of Bliss* (Trafalgar Studios); *Breakfast with Mugabe* (Theatre Royal Bath); *Someone Who'll Watch Over Me* (Theatre Royal Northampton) and Olivier Award-winner *The Mountaintop, Inches Apart, Ship of Fools, Natural Selection* and *Salt Meets Wound* (Theatre503).

Television includes *Ripper Street, Agatha Christie's Marple, No Win No Fee, Sex 'N' Death, Wipeout* and *The Ship*.

Orchestration includes *Agatha Christie's Marple, Primeval, Dracula, Jericho, If I Had You, A History of Britain, Silent Witness, Dalziel and Pascoe, Alice Through the Looking Glass, The Nine Lives of Tomas Katz* and *Scenes of a Sexual Nature*.

Interactive and digital work includes *You Shall Go To The Ball* (Royal Opera House); *Light* (BAC); *Foundling Museum* (The Foundling Museum, London) and *Moore Outside* (Tate Britain/Coney).

Chris Foxon | Producer

Chris joined Papatango in 2012 and his productions with the company include *Orca* (Papatango New Writing Prize 2016, Southwark Playhouse), *After Independence* (Arcola Theatre, 2016 Alfred Fagon Audience Award), *Tomcat* (Papatango New Writing Prize 2015, Southwark Playhouse), *Coolatully* (Papatango New Writing Prize 2014, Finborough Theatre), *Unscorched* (Papatango New Writing Prize 2013, Finborough Theatre), and *Pack* and *Everyday Maps for Everyday Use* (Papatango New Writing Prize 2012, Finborough Theatre).

His other productions include *The Transatlantic Commissions* (Old Vic Theatre); *Donkey Heart* (Old Red Lion Theatre/Trafalgar Studios); *The Fear of Breathing* (Finborough Theatre; transferred in a new production to the Akasaka Red Theatre, Tokyo); *The Keepers of Infinite Space* (Park Theatre); *Happy New* (Trafalgar Studios); *Tejas Verdes* (Edinburgh Festival) and *The Madness of George III* (Oxford Playhouse).

Chris is a visiting lecturer at the Royal Central School of Speech and Drama and the University of York. He is co-writing *Being A Playwright: A Career Guide For Writers*, due for publication in 2018.

George Turvey | Dramaturg

George co-founded Papatango in 2007 and became the sole Artistic Director in January 2013.

Credits as director include *The Annihilation of Jessie Leadbeater* (Papatango at ALRA), *After Independence* (Papatango at Arcola Theatre, 2016 Alfred Fagon Audience Award), *Leopoldville* (Papatango at Tristan Bates Theatre) and *Angel* (Papatango at Pleasance London and Tristan Bates Theatre).

George trained as an actor at the Academy of Live and Recorded Arts (ALRA) and has appeared on stage and screen throughout the UK and internationally, including the lead roles in the world premiere of Arthur Miller's *No Villain* (Old Red Lion Theatre and Trafalgar Studios) and *Batman Live World Arena Tour*.

As a dramaturg, he has led the development of all of Papatango's productions. He is co-writing *Being A Playwright: A Career Guide For Writers*, due for publication in 2018.

Production Acknowledgements

Papatango New Writing Prize Reading Team | **David K. Barnes, Kate Brower, Michael Byrne, Alexandra Coke, Sam Donovan, Katie Ebner-Landy, Maddy Hill, Jonny Kelly, Justine Malone, Bethany Pitts, Matt Roberts, Tamar Saphra, Imogen Sarre, Emily Standring, Roisin Symes, Rosie Wyatt**

Image Design | **Rebecca Pitt**

Production Photography | **Robert Workman**

Press Representation | **Kate Morley PR**

Many thanks to our generous supporters: Arts Council England, Backstage Trust, Boris Karloff Charitable Foundation, Garfield Weston Foundation, Golsoncott Foundation, Harold Hyam Wingate Foundation, Mildred Duveen Charitable Trust, Leche Trust, and Kathryn Thompson.

We are very grateful to our post-show event partners: The Loss Foundation and Dr Erin Hope Thompson, Professor Debora Price of The Manchester Institute for Collaborative Research on Ageing (MICRA), Professor Sarah Harper of The Oxford Institute of Population Ageing, Dr Kellie Payne of the Campaign to End Loneliness, and the Jo Cox Commission on Loneliness.

This production has been licensed by arrangement with The Agency (London) Ltd, 24 Pottery Lane, London, W11 4LZ. Email: info@theagency.co.uk.

The Loss Foundation is the only UK charity dedicated solely to providing bereavement support following the loss of a loved one to cancer, whether that be spouses, family members, friends or colleagues. The Foundation provides a variety of support events to help people at any point during their loss, and create the opportunity to meet others who have experienced something similar. They also undertake research, and educate and empower others to support those who are grieving via workshops and training. **www.thelossfoundation.org**

The Oxford Institute of Population Ageing was established in 1998. Based on the US Population Center, it was funded by a grant from the National Institute of Health (National Institute on Aging – NIA) to establish the UK's first population centre on the demography and economics of ageing populations. Our aim is to undertake research into the implications of population change. We are a multi-disciplinary group with demography as our main disciplinary focus. Our researchers work in Africa, Latin America, Asia and Europe, and we run the Population Networks AFRAN (Africa), LARNA (Latin America), and EAST (Central and Eastern Europe).

The University of Manchester
Institute for Collaborative
Research on Ageing

Situated in the heart of Manchester, the UK's first city to achieve World Health Organization 'Age-Friendly' status, the **University of Manchester's Institute for Collaborative Research on Ageing** is one of the country's leading research institutes in the field of human ageing and ageing populations. Our researchers address fundamental questions about ageing and society through multidisciplinary research across the humanities, the arts and the sciences.

'Remarkable unearthers of new talent' *Evening Standard*

Papatango discover and champion new playwrights through free, open application schemes and opportunities.

Our flagship programme is the Papatango New Writing Prize, the UK's only annual award guaranteeing an emerging playwright a full production, publication, 10% of the gross box office, and an unprecedented £6000 commission for a second play. The Prize is free to enter and assessed anonymously, and all entrants receive personal feedback on their scripts, an unmatched commitment to supporting aspiring playwrights. Over 1000 entries are received each year.

Writers discovered through the Prize have received Off West End and RNT Foundation Playwright Awards and BAFTAs, made work with the RSC, BBC, Hampstead Theatre, National Theatre, Out of Joint and other leading organisations, and premiered in over twenty countries.

Papatango also run an annual Resident Playwright scheme, taking an emerging playwright through commissioning, development and production of a new play. Our first Resident, May Sumbwanyambe, won the 2016 Alfred Fagon Audience Award for our production of *After Independence*, which we then adapted and produced for BBC Radio Four. Our second Resident, Samantha Potter, won a place on the Channel 4 Playwright's Scheme with our backing, and will see Papatango tour her play *Hanna* nationwide in 2018.

Papatango launched a new arm in summer 2017 called GoWrite. GoWrite delivers an extensive programme of free playwriting opportunities for children and adults nationwide. Children in state schools write their own plays which are then professionally performed and published, while adults take part in workshops, complete six-month courses at a variety of regional venues culminating in free public performances, or join fortnightly one-to-one career facilitation services. GoWrite has delivered face-to-face training for over 2000 budding writers this year alone, with £5000 available in bursaries to enable in-need writers nationwide to access our opportunities.

10% of seats at our productions are donated to charities for young people at risk of exclusion from the arts.

All our opportunities are free and entered anonymously, encouraging the best new talent regardless of means or connections.

Papatango's motto is simple. All you need is a story.

Papatango are a registered charity.

We rely on the generous support of individuals, as well as trusts and foundations, to deliver our unprecedented and unmatched programme of free opportunities for aspiring playwrights otherwise at risk of exclusion from theatre. Any donation helps us to ensure that the success of our discoveries inspires grassroots writers of all ages that they too can break into theatre. All they need is a story.

If you would like to support Papatango or perhaps get involved in a particular project, then please email **chris@papatango.co.uk**.

We make a little go a long way.

£5 buys a ticket for an in-need young person

£10 covers the cost of printing scripts for an entire cast

£20 funds the resources for a free writing workshop

£50 provides 25 free playtexts for school libraries

£75 pays for a day of rehearsals

£100 provides a full costume for a character on stage

£200 enables us to travel to run workshops across the UK

£500 pays for a special performance for a school group

£1000 funds a week of script R&D with actors and writer

£2000 supports a budding writer with a seed commission

£6000 commissions a full script from a new writer

£10,000 pays for a brilliant cast for a month-long show

Every donation makes an enormous difference.

Online
For up-to-date news and opportunities please visit:
www.facebook.com/pages/PapaTango-Theatre-Company/257825071298
www.twitter.com/PapaTangoTC
www.papatango.co.uk

Papatango Theatre Company Ltd is a registered charity and a company limited by guarantee. Registered in England and Wales no. 07365398. Registered Charity no. 1152789.

'Southwark Playhouse churn out arresting productions at a rate of knots' *Time Out*

Southwark Playhouse is all about telling stories and inspiring the next generation of storytellers and theatre makers. It aims to facilitate the work of new and emerging theatre practitioners from early in their creative lives to the start of their professional careers.

Through our schools work we aim to introduce local people at a young age to the possibilities of great drama and the benefits of using theatre skills to facilitate learning. Each year we engage with over 5,000 school pupils through free schools performances and long-term in school curriculum support.

Through our participation programmes we aim to work with all members of our local community in a wide-ranging array of creative drama projects that aim to promote cohesion, build confidence and encourage a lifelong appreciation of theatre.

Our theatre programme aims to facilitate and showcase the work of some of the UK's best up and coming talent with a focus on reinterpreting classic plays and contemporary plays of note. Our two atmospheric theatre spaces enable us to offer theatre artists and companies the opportunity to present their first fully realised productions. Over the past twenty-four years we have produced and presented early productions by many aspiring theatre practitioners many of whom are now enjoying flourishing careers.

'A brand as quirky as it is classy' *The Stage*

For more information about our forthcoming season and to book tickets visit www.southwarkplayhouse.co.uk. You can also support us online by joining our Facebook and Twitter pages.

Staff List

Patrons Sir Michael Caine, Sir Simon Hughes, Andy Serkis

Board of Trustees Sarah Hickson, Rodney Pearson, Joe Roberts, Giles Semper, Kathryn Serkis, Glenn Wellman, Tim Wood (chair)

Theatre Manager Joe Deighan

Assistant Technical Manager Lee Elston

Assistant Theatre Manager Sophie Quaile

Technical Manager Christopher Randall

General Manager Corinne Beaver

Press & Publicity Manager Susie Safavi

Artistic Director (CEO) Chris Smyrnios

Box Office & Sales Coordinator Charlotte Spencer

Youth & Community Director David Workman

TRESTLE

Stewart Pringle

Acknowledgements

Thanks to friends who read kindly and noted wisely: Adam
Hughes, Duncan Gates, Will Young, Tom Richards, Jeffrey
Mayhew, George Warren and Tim Foley. To my wonderful (and
v. patient) agent Jonathan. To George and Chris from Papatango,
to Cathal, Eddie and the whole *Trestle* team who have made
every step of this journey such a joy. To the Southwark Playhouse
and all who sail in her. To Matt, John, Sarah Liisa and all at Nick
Hern Books. To Ellie, Madani, Omar and the team at the Bush
Theatre for the support and headspace needed for this.

Thanks-beyond-thanks to Lauren, none of this would be possible
without you and your constant faith, love and brilliance.

And finally to my peculiar and perfect family, who never ask
when I'm planning to grow up, and who taught me that every
day is a special occasion.

S.P.

To Mike Fry,
without whom none of this would be preferable

Characters

HARRY
DENISE

Scenes take place at intervals of a week unless otherwise
indicated.

A forward slash (/) indicates the next line is to interrupt the
current one.

Words in [square brackets] are unspoken or almost spoken.

Line breaks in the text denote a pause or silence.

Lines that end without punctuation indicate an incompleteness
or hesitance.

*This text went to press before the end of rehearsals and so may
differ slightly from the play as performed.*

1.

A Temperance Hall in a small Yorkshire village. It is the present day. There are blackboards, pinboards peppered with notices and a wheel for displaying the trump suit in whist.

HARRY *is a man in his mid- to late sixties. He sits at a trestle table covered in various heaps of paper, and a gavel. There are a number of stackable chairs in front of it.*

He's laughing gently as he sorts the papers into his briefcase, and puts on his coat.

DENISE *enters, unseen. She is also in her sixties, and she carries a large wheelie bag.*

HARRY   I do declare…

           Mumbles under breath.

           …are at an end.

           Mimes banging gavel.

           Mumbles.

           …are closed.

           Mimes banging gavel again.

           I do declare –

DENISE   Yes?

HARRY   Sorry. Oh, sorry. I was. Yes. Never mind.

DENISE   Oh, I don't mind.

HARRY   No, of course.
           Just packing up.

DENISE   That's fine.

HARRY   Hand with the?

DENISE   Sorry?

HARRY   Table.
           Shall I –

DENISE   Alright then.
           Thank you.

           They flip the table upside down and HARRY
           undoes the legs on his side. DENISE *struggles with*
           hers. He waits for her.

HARRY   Do you –

DENISE   Almost.

           More struggling. DENISE *tugging at it now. More*
           struggling.

HARRY   Let me.

           DENISE *manages it.*

           Where's it going? Just against the wall?

DENISE   That'll be fine, yes.

           They move the table against the wall.

HARRY   Bye then.

           Picks up suitcase to leave.

DENISE   Bye.
           You're new then?

HARRY   No, but you are.

DENISE   I'm not new. And I've never seen you before.

HARRY   Well, you must be quite new, because I've never
           seen you before.

DENISE   I've been here six months.

HARRY   Six months is new.
           Six months is very new. I've been coming here
           ten years.
           I've been Chair for four.
           I'm not new. You're new.

DENISE   I've just never seen you before. It's usually empty
           Thursdays.

HARRY   Six months and you're telling me what's 'usually'.

DENISE   That what the hammer's for?

HARRY   The what? The. Oh, yes.
           Good –

DENISE   Did they buy it for you?

HARRY   Did who buy what? Yes, no they didn't. Look, you
           are alright to do the chairs, aren't you?
           The last.
           She did the chairs.
           Will you?

DENISE   Oh I don't do chairs.

HARRY   Well. Ha. What do you do?
           It's all chairs. All there is is chairs.
           Sorry, but if I'd known I'd have asked for some help.
           If I'd known, but

DENISE   Right.

HARRY   Don't you do them?
           It's just that it's quite frustrating. First the kitchen

DENISE   The kitchen's closed.

HARRY   Yes.

DENISE   The sink's backed up.

HARRY   I know the kitchen's closed, there's a sign.
           So first the kitchen

DENISE   Been out all summer.

HARRY   And now the chairs. It's not free.

DENISE   No

HARRY   It's five pounds an hour.
           And I'm thinking.
           What I'm starting to think now.

Is what
What am I paying for?
With my five pounds. Do you see?

DENISE   Yes, I can see that.
          Sorry about that.

HARRY   So can't you just do the chairs?

DENISE   I don't mind helping.

HARRY   Helping?

DENISE   There aren't many.

          Starts stacking chairs.

HARRY   So you won't do the chairs?

DENISE   I will, I'll help.

HARRY   That's not what I
          So what do you do if you don't do chairs?

DENISE   Zumba.

HARRY   Oh God
          Oh God I'm so sorry!

          Runs to help.

          So so sorry.
          I thought.

DENISE   I know what you thought, it's this coat, I don't mind.

HARRY   Let me.

DENISE   I thought that when I bought it.

HARRY   Please.

DENISE   It's done.

HARRY   No, let me.

DENISE   It's done.
          There.

HARRY   Sorry.
          I'm Harry.

DENISE   Hello Harry.

           I've got to set up.

HARRY   Fine.

DENISE   Bye.

HARRY   Right.

           HARRY *leaves. Blackout.*

2.

HARRY *is stacking the last of the chairs.* DENISE *enters.*

DENISE   Oh.

HARRY   Ta-da!

DENISE   Well, that's...

HARRY   Not a problem.

DENISE   Thank you.

HARRY   Say no more. I shaved five minutes off the
           treasurer's closing address.

DENISE   You shouldn't have...

HARRY   Glad to. He's goes on a bit.
           Could happily have shaved off five more but he did
           a bit about Mrs Henshaw –

DENISE   She's died.

HARRY   – who's died and so I worried it'd sound a bit off.

DENISE   Of course.

HARRY   So I thought.
           Sorry again.

DENISE   Nothing to be sorry for. It's that coat.

HARRY   Nothing wrong with your coat.

DENISE   I said to myself 'If that's the message this coat's
          sending out'

HARRY   It wasn't!

DENISE   'If it's sending out a "cleaner" sort of message…'

HARRY   No, no.

DENISE   Then I'm not sure it's the right coat for me at all.

HARRY   It was just the timing, that's all. I didn't have my
          specs on.

DENISE   Anyway, I've burned it.

HARRY   You've what?

DENISE   Burned it in the garden. Straight when I got home.

HARRY   In the garden?

DENISE   Whoof! Went up like a balloon.
          That's polyester for you.

HARRY   Hmm.
          Ha! Ah-ha!
          That was a joke wasn't it?

DENISE   It was, yeah.

HARRY   Very funny.
          Very funny, that.
          Whoof!

          Anyway, I've done you the chairs.

          Blackout.

3.

DENISE *is alone and warming up, stretching. She goes to her bag and removes a small tape deck. Checks the tape, turns it over, switches it on. 'Drop It Low' by Ester Dean. She goes back to warming up. Quite vigorously.*

HARRY *enters. Watches for a while.* DENISE *is grunting slightly as she stretches.*

HARRY	Sorry
DENISE	Jesus!
HARRY	I've left my
DENISE	Thought you'd gone
HARRY	I've left my I think my coat is
DENISE	It's ten-past
HARRY	It's just my coat, I've left it in the
DENISE	Right
HARRY	I'll just
DENISE	If you don't mind.
HARRY	Sorry
DENISE	It's fine.

HARRY *retrieves his coat from a peg on the wall.* DENISE *goes to the tape player and turns it off.*

HARRY	You listen to that?
DENISE	Not really. But you can't really work out to Brahms can you?
HARRY	You like Brahms?
DENISE	No. I like EDM.

That was Ester Jane featuring Chris Brown.

HARRY   Right.

DENISE   He punched his wife.

HARRY   That's awful.

DENISE   Well, girlfriend –

HARRY   Still

DENISE   – but he's largely been forgiven.

HARRY   Right.
Right.

Just sounds like noise to me, I'm afraid.

DENISE   Really?

HARRY   Erm
Yes
Yes

I'm Harry, by the way.

DENISE   I know. You told me.

HARRY   Ah. Yes. Sorry.
And you are –

DENISE   Denise.

HARRY   Denise from Zumba.
How is it going?

DENISE   The Zumba?

HARRY   Any of it.

DENISE   It's alright.

HARRY   Was everything alright with
The room
Left it alright for you?

DENISE   Left it fine, thank you.

HARRY   And the temperature

DENISE   Temperature's fine

HARRY   Not too cold

DENISE   Too warm, if anything.

HARRY   You won't be saying that in November, let me
           tell you.

DENISE   I daresay.

           They'll be here in a minute.
           Just have to get set up.

HARRY   Of course.

           Sorry. Of course.

           *HARRY goes to leave. Halfway through the door
           he turns back, turns on the tape player. Exits.*

           Blackout.

4.

*HARRY is alone, wrestling with his mobile phone. The chairs
have been cleared,* DENISE*'s wheelie bag is already in the
room.* DENISE *enters.*

DENISE   Thank you for staying on.

HARRY   Not at all.
           I think it's quite ridiculous.

DENISE   So do I.

HARRY   The kitchen
           I think the kitchen is ridiculous
           But to not have a working toilet in the whole place.

DENISE   It's a nuisance.

HARRY   It is a nuisance.
           It's a real nuisance.
           And at five pounds an hour

DENISE   You expect a working loo.

HARRY   You do. It's just laziness.
           I mean I don't mind going
           Across the road, or whatever
           But for you all

DENISE   Oh we manage

HARRY   Did he say anything to you?

DENISE   No, he was fine, I know him.

HARRY   Really?

DENISE   I go in there sometimes after class.

HARRY   In The Kentish Drover?

DENISE   In The Drover, yes.

HARRY   I'd not been in for [years]
           Not sure I'll be back.

DENISE   Did he say anything to you?

HARRY   Nothing to me. But he
           He apparently gave Gerald
           Gerald's the Social Secretary
           He apparently gave Gerald
           You know.
           A look.

DENISE   What sort of look?

HARRY   Just a
           Just a look.
           I wasn't actually there, and he was perfectly civil
           to me.

DENISE   But he gave Gerald a look?

HARRY   Apparently.

DENISE   He's alright, the landlord.

HARRY   If you say so.

DENISE   Maybe Gerald

HARRY   Maybe Gerald what?

DENISE   Well maybe Gerald was a bit rude to him.

HARRY   Do you know Gerald?

DENISE   No.

HARRY   Well there you are then.
You don't know Gerald.

DENISE   Alright.

HARRY   He's not the rude

DENISE   Alright.

Would you like a hand with that?
Mine's, em

HARRY   What?
(*The phone*.)
Yes.

HARRY *hands her the phone*.

I'm just trying to
I don't know.

DENISE   It's on flight mode.

HARRY   Probably.

DENISE   Not flying home, are you?

HARRY   No
No I've brought the car.

DENISE   Course.

Hands phone back.

HARRY   Thank you
Wonderful.

DENISE   Well I'd best get
You know

HARRY   Of course, sorry.

DENISE   They'll be late.

HARRY   Will they?

DENISE   They're always late

HARRY   What a nuisance

DENISE   Oh I don't mind.

HARRY   Don't you?

DENISE   No.
I don't mind a bit.

DENISE *smiles*.

Blackout.

5.

DENISE *has a plastic bag by her feet. She is eating a sandwich and talking to* HARRY.

DENISE   I've hardly had anything all day, so I'm starved.
I haven't had a chance to sit down, and I've only
popped in for a minute because it's not the weather
for sitting outside and anyway if you don't use
them then you lose them, that's what I've always
said. And I don't eat breakfasts, never have.
Anyway, I'm sitting there, minding my own
business, and I get out a banana. And I'm sitting
there, and I'm peeling it, and I'm not paying in the
least attention to anyone because I've got my
Hilary Mantel and the library's almost empty
anyway and that's when he pipes up. 'You can
smell a banana, can't you?' You can smell a
banana! And I look up and he's not speaking to
me, and there's nobody else in the vicinity so he's
just actually saying it to himself. But I know it's
for my benefit so I finish the bite I'm on and I put
it away, and after that I can't get back into my
Hilary for blushing and so a few minutes later
I leave. And as I'm leaving I think, 'You mouse,
Denise. You're a mouse.' And I'm so cross with

myself, and with him. That I go back inside and tell him what I think of him.

Almost.

I mean, I didn't, but I should have. I wish I had.

I just don't think he had any right to make me feel that

Shit

Do you?

'You can smell a banana.'

So, I mean. You don't mind me having this, do you?

HARRY   No. Not at all.

DENISE   Magic.

Blackout.

6.

DENISE *is helping* HARRY *with a table or a chair.* DENISE *is eating a sandwich.*

DENISE   She's gone up to his apartment, to his office, except it's got a bed in it. A bed in his office!

HARRY   Crikey.

DENISE   Behind a filing cabinet or whatever, he's got a full bed laid out. And so he's –

HARRY   Lift the...

DENISE   – all 'Come into my bed office', and so she does. And bearing in mind she's about –

HARRY   Mind the

DENISE   – twenty against his easily thirty-five. And five minutes later he's got her tied up like a scarecrow

with tits against the end of his bed. And he's
blindfolded her and he's going –

HARRY   Can you just

DENISE   – south. If you know what I mean. And then he's
on top and he's just banging –

HARRY   And lift

DENISE   – away at her. For about thirty seconds. And that's
about it, in the way of sex. The rest's just

blather.

HARRY   I still think I won't bother.

DENISE   I wouldn't. I'd give it a miss.

HARRY   Are you enjoying that?

DENISE   Yes, thank you.

HARRY   Is it

DENISE   You'll not guess it. It's pastrami ham and
wholegrain mustard.

HARRY   Lovely.

DENISE   You had pastrami?

HARRY   Oh yes.

           Doesn't it bother your
           You know
           Before all that jumping about?

DENISE   Jumping about?

HARRY   The

DENISE   It's not jumping about, Harry. It's Zumba.

HARRY   I've never seen it, I must admit.

DENISE   You should give it a go?

HARRY   You think?

DENISE   No.

HARRY   Oh.

DENISE   I'm teasing, you give it a go if you want to.

HARRY   I've got arthritis so

DENISE   Be good for arthritis
           Probably.

HARRY   Still, I.
           Best not.

           Right then
           Cheerio.

           Enjoy your jumping about.

DENISE   Ah!

           (*Cheeky.*) Bye, Harry.

           Blackout.

7.

DENISE *is shutting the door.*

DENISE   Ta-ta, then!

HARRY   Sorry about that
           You're early.

DENISE   Nothing to be sorry for
           Nice to see some faces.

           Good to know you're not just turning up here on
           your own.

           Like a creep.

           It'd be dead creepy that wouldn't it?
           If you'd said you were in a whatever but really
           Really it was just you turning up here
           With your papers

           Or if all the others were dead.

HARRY   Dead?

DENISE   If they were all just
          Dead
          And you just sat there
          Like their king.

HARRY   How would that work then?

DENISE   I'm just glad to see you've got some friends,
          that's all
          Christ

          I didn't actually recognise anyone.
          Apart from Kevin from the butcher's
          Was that Kevin?

HARRY   It was.

DENISE   Apart from Kevin I didn't actually recognise
          anyone.
          And I know everyone.

HARRY   I've got friends

DENISE   I knew it was.

          Sorry?

HARRY   I've got friends, Denise

          I'm a widower I'm not Dracula

DENISE   I know that, I know that
          But I mean.

          Like, friends friends.
          Not just this lot

HARRY   Some of this lot are my friends

DENISE   Seriously?

HARRY   Some of them
          But anyway
          I have all sorts of friends.

DENISE   Of course you do.

HARRY   And what's wrong with 'this lot'?

DENISE   Nothing.

HARRY   How do you mean you know everyone?

DENISE   It's hardly a metropolis.

HARRY   Did you know me?
           Before, I mean.

DENISE   I'd seen you around.
           Noticed from a distance.

HARRY   Oh
           Oh right, good.

DENISE   Had you notic–

HARRY   No.

DENISE   Oh

HARRY   Sorry, I just

DENISE   No, why would you?

           I just wondered
           I suppose
           Why you always stay on here.

HARRY   Oh
           It's just
           It's nice to chat, isn't it?
           Nice to be sociable.

DENISE   It is.

HARRY   I've actually
           I've brought

           HARRY *takes some wrapped sandwiches from his bag*.

           I thought
           If you didn't mind?

DENISE   No!
           No, that'd be nice.

HARRY   Great.
           Shall we?

           Blackout.

8.

HARRY *and* DENISE *at either side of the table.*

DENISE   Two... one... and

HARRY   That's it.

          Table legs snapped down in unison.

          Let me.

          HARRY *stacks the table against the wall. Sorts his
          things.*

DENISE   Good turn-out.

HARRY   Would you say so?

DENISE   Looked like it.

HARRY   Well

DENISE   It's not everyone's thing is it
          Politics
          Not round here anyway.

HARRY   True enough
          I mean to say, that's what we're working on.

DENISE   Nobody wants to get involved do they
          Nobody wants to speak up.
          Not supposed to have an opinion if you've got
          a bus pass.

HARRY   People don't listen
          Don't want to hear it.

DENISE   I know exactly what you mean.

          Is this yours?

          DENISE *is holding* HARRY*'s gavel.*

HARRY   No!
          Yes, well
          It belongs to the
          But it's mine.

DENISE   You're the Chair?

HARRY   That's right

DENISE   So they gave you a hammer?

HARRY   Gavel

DENISE   Do you bang it?
Do you bang your hammer?

HARRY   Not
Not really
Sometimes.

Anyway, have a good Zumba

DENISE   Thank you Harry.

HARRY   Ta-ta now.

DENISE   Bye.

HARRY   Actually
Actually as a matter of fact I bought it
On eBay

And I've never banged it
I've never banged it once

DENISE *smiles, so does* HARRY.

Blackout.

9.

HARRY *and* DENISE *are both sat on the trestle table, eating their sandwiches.*

HARRY   I help out there Mondays, which is all day
          It's easy stuff if you've got a bit of training in the
          legal side of things
          And I have
          It's just forms that people can't be bothered to do
          themselves
          It's all on the Google anyway
          It's more or less just being paid to do the Google,
          these days
          But you have to know where to look and that's
          where
          That's where the little bit of legal training's
          invaluable
          Tuesdays whist, and that used to be here but it's
          hardly worth it for two tables and so that's just
          round at whoever it happens to be that week.
          Wednesday I'm back at the CAB all day.
          Thursdays getting ready for here and then here.
          Fridays I sometimes go to the pub, if there's no
          sports on.

DENISE   Right

HARRY   Saturdays depends but it's usually Gyffords if I have
          something to pick up, you know
          Sundays I do a roast or I go to a roast.

DENISE   Lovely

HARRY   Then it just starts again, you know.

DENISE   I can imagine.

HARRY   Sorry.
          That was a bit more than you asked for, wasn't it?

DENISE   No, it was interesting.

HARRY   Sorry

          What do you, em

DENISE   I read.

HARRY   Right.

DENISE   Voracious.
          I've got a book group.

HARRY   Really?

DENISE   You don't have to sound quite so surprised.

HARRY   I'm not surprised
          It's good
          What are you, you know
          At the moment?

DENISE   *Captain Corelli's Mandolin.*

HARRY   Lovely.

DENISE   You've read it?

HARRY   Not as such, no.

DENISE   There was quite a good blue bit in the film but
          they've cut it out the book.
          Prudes.

HARRY   That's a shame.

DENISE   Isn't it?
          I was quite disappointed, I told them.

HARRY   Did they laugh?

DENISE   How do you mean?

HARRY   I just thought they might have.

DENISE   Well they didn't.

          Here

          DENISE *hands* HARRY *a piece of her sandwich.*

          Guess

HARRY   Guess?

DENISE   Guess
          Guess my sandwich

HARRY *sniffs it. Not nice. Takes a bite.*

HARRY   Mmm.

DENISE   Mmm?

HARRY   It's
           Sorry

           Chewing.

           It's

DENISE   It's?

HARRY   It's
           Horrible

           What the bloody hell is it?

DENISE   Pickle and pesto

HARRY   That's demented
           They're both spreads.

DENISE   So?

HARRY   You can't have two spreads

DENISE   I can
           I just have.

HARRY   You're a rebel

DENISE   I'm a rebel without a cause
           Roaming the countryside
           Using two spreads at once

           Come on then

HARRY   Come on what?

DENISE   Pass it over

           HARRY *passes a chunk of sandwich to* DENISE.
           She eats it.

           That's good

HARRY   That's beef

DENISE   That's really good

HARRY   Thank you

DENISE   You cooked this?

HARRY   I did.
          Cooked it on Sunday.

DENISE   It's good
          Really good

HARRY   Secret?

DENISE   Mmm-hmm

HARRY   Honey.

DENISE   Honey?

HARRY   Fresh honey.

DENISE   From bees?

HARRY   From bees.

DENISE   You keep bees?
          I love bees
          Do you keep bees?

HARRY   No
          It's from Sainsbury's but

          Originally

DENISE   Well, it's really
          Really
          Really nice.

          Pause.

HARRY   Thank you.

          Pause.

DENISE   Right
          I'm off for my wee.

HARRY   Oh. Sorry.

DENISE   You're sorry for my wee?

HARRY   No no, I just meant

DENISE   If I don't have my wee I'll never enjoy it.
          It hurts if you don't have a wee.

HARRY   Oh right, yes.
          Well hope it goes
          Yes.

          Blackout.

10.

DENISE *eats a banana, alone. After a moment,* HARRY *enters with two cups of tea.*

DENISE   My hero!
          What spoils hath thou brought me?
          Hast thou vanquished the evil tea urn?

HARRY   I... hast
          Or, no, I've just
          There's a kettle.

DENISE   Oh well, still.

HARRY   Handle! It's hot

DENISE   Lovely.

HARRY   A bit more civilised than a flask.

DENISE   I'll say.

HARRY   Brian brings a flask full of
          Something
          To the meetings
          It's not tea, or not what I'd call tea.

DENISE   Not Yorkshire Tea.

HARRY   Not Yorkshire Tea, no.
          But now there's a kettle.

DENISE   Much better.

HARRY *goes to a carrier bag at the back of the hall.*

HARRY   Now, put that down.

DENISE   Pardon?

HARRY   Just put it down, just for a minute.

DENISE   Why?

HARRY   Just do what I say.

DENISE   Alright.

HARRY   Don't turn round.

DENISE   Eh?

HARRY   Don't turn round, I said.
Surprise.

DENISE   Another surprise?
Harry I'm a sixty-three-year-old woman, another surprise on top of the Yorkshire Tea and I'm liable for a turn.

HARRY   Hang on. Look straight ahead.

DENISE   Right.

HARRY *produces a black silk scarf from his bag, approaches* DENISE *and ties it round her eyes.*

HARRY   There.

DENISE   Harry what the fuck are you doing?

HARRY   Leave it

DENISE   What are you doing?

HARRY   Stay there

DENISE   Harry?

HARRY   Hands by your sides.

DENISE *obeys, disconcerted.*

Open your mouth.

DENISE   Are you fuck–

            HARRY stuffs the corner of a sandwich into her mouth. She almost gags.

HARRY   Guess!

DENISE   You
           Fucki–
           Mm

HARRY   Stop talking you'll choke yourself.

DENISE   You're a –

           Cheese and onion.

HARRY   You've got it!

DENISE   Jesus Christ.

            HARRY pulls off the blindfold.

HARRY   Now you do me.

           What?

DENISE   I thought you were
           Well it doesn't really matter what I thought you were doing but thank God you're not doing it.

HARRY   Oh
           Oh!
           This is the Temperance Hall not Shades of whatever

DENISE   I know!

HARRY   My mam used to run the bake sale here!

DENISE   I'm sure she did!

HARRY   It's just not that sort of place
           At all.

DENISE   Fine!

HARRY   Mind you.

DENISE   What?

HARRY   Well...
         The Lions.

DENISE   What of them?

HARRY   You hear things about The Lions, don't you?

DENISE   I hear when they're having a ceilidh.
         I hear about their Shakespeare evenings when Ruth
         gets up in a ruff and does the balcony bit from
         Romeo and Juliet with Foley who does the wood-
         carving.
         I hear a lot about that.

HARRY   I hear a lot more than just that.

DENISE   From who?

HARRY   Just about.

DENISE   You're an old woman.

HARRY   Well I'd rather be an old woman than a

DENISE   Lion

HARRY   Well I would!
         They think it's all
         London.
         They're mostly from London and they think this is
         just a sort of London as well and they can just do as
         they please.

DENISE   Well they can!

HARRY   Of course they can! Just leave me out of it
         That's all I'm saying.
         What?
         You're laughing at me.

DENISE   I'm not.
         Sorry.
         Do you mind awfully?

HARRY   No
         I'm not sure that I do.

         Blackout.

11.

DENISE *enters with her bag. She looks around, but the room is empty and the table is collapsed against the wall.*

She removes her tape player from her bag, presses play.

Blackout.

12.

HARRY *is hurriedly filling his bag with papers. Then he begins to tackle the erected trestle table on his own, but struggles. Collapses one leg. He traps his hand in it.*

HARRY   Ah! Bugger!

          Collapses the other leg. DENISE *enters.*

DENISE   Do you want a

HARRY   No, no.
          Got it.

          HARRY *struggles to sort the table and stack it against the wall.*

          Night

          Goes to collect things.

DENISE   You going then?

HARRY   Yes
          I've got to
          There's.
          Stuff

DENISE   Oh, alright, yeah

HARRY   Cheerio

DENISE   Harry?

HARRY   Yes, what?

DENISE   Stop smiling

HARRY   I'm not smiling!

DENISE   You are
           You're smiling and it's weird

HARRY   No, it's not

DENISE   It is though.

           You're not really a smiler
           Are you?

           Where were you last week?

HARRY   Nowhere
           Home
           Finished early.

DENISE   Right

           Look, don't be like this.

HARRY   I'm not being like anything.

DENISE   I thought you knew

HARRY   Knew what?

DENISE   I thought I'd said
           I'm sure I'd said

HARRY   You hadn't.

DENISE   No
           I suppose not.

HARRY   And there's no

           Indicates his ring finger.

           So

DENISE   I've got a nickel allergy.

HARRY   A what?

DENISE   It's a kind of dermatitis, so I can't [wear one]

HARRY   Right.
           Anyway, it doesn't matter!

DENISE   Doesn't it?

HARRY   No
Of course it doesn't!

I only
I only called because of the keys

App
App-arently you've been just leaving the keys
under the mat
When you leave

DENISE   That was what I was

HARRY   Well, you mustn't
It isn't safe
We've had break-ins in the past

DENISE   Rubbish
A pigeon is not a break-in, Harry

HARRY   We've had problems with it in the past
It's not as safe as you think and anyway
Anyway, you're to deliver the key back to the
designated warden at the end of your session

I'm not making a fuss about it!

DENISE   You patently are

HARRY   And anyway you didn't
Say.

Pause.

DENISE   Sorry.

I just

You hadn't said anything and it just got past the
time to

HARRY   It doesn't matter

DENISE   Well it does if it's upset you
I just thought you were lonely

HARRY   Oh thanks very much!
Lonely!
Look, there's only one lonely one here and that's

I'm not

Look I called about the key and now it's said

DENISE   It's nothing.
I explained

HARRY   Oh did you?
That's champion that is
Explained.

DENISE   He didn't mind
He thought.

HARRY   He thought what?

DENISE   Nothing.

HARRY   I'd hope
There's
I mean
There's nothing to mind.

DENISE   No.

HARRY   Is there?

DENISE   There's nothing to mind.

There's nothing.

Blackout.

13.

HARRY has collapsed the table and is setting it against the wall. He's in a hurry. He takes a bunch of flowers out of a carrier bag, and picks a price tag off its wrapper. Takes a card out of the bag, finds a pen, writes it out. Puts the flowers in the middle of the room, card propped on them.

Adjusts them.
Adjusts them again.

Fetches a chair and puts it in the centre of the room, puts the flowers on it.

DENISE enters quietly, watches him for a moment.

DENISE   I don't think so.

HARRY   Ah!

DENISE   You can't just leave them there.
          It looks mental.

HARRY   I'll be off.

DENISE   There's no need to

HARRY   No, no

DENISE   Don't rush off.
          Look at me.

HARRY   See you soon.

DENISE   Look at me!

          He does.

          You're a silly sod.

          Those for me?
          I hate flowers.

HARRY   Oh
          Sorry, I

DENISE   Of course I don't hate flowers
          Nobody hates flowers

          Thank you, Harry.

HARRY   My pleasure.

DENISE   I thought you might have topped yourself actually

HARRY   Right

DENISE   You have a look of it

HARRY   Like I might kill myself

DENISE   At any moment, yeah.
           I think I'd have thought that was quite sexy
           If you'd just gone 'Oh, she's spoken for, I must'
           (*Sound and mime of shooting herself in the head.*)
           You know.

HARRY   I just felt a bit of a fool
           So I thought I'd best.

           Anyway, I'm off.

           Friends?

DENISE   Maybe.

HARRY   Maybe

DENISE   What if I want something else?

HARRY   What do you mean?

DENISE   I want you to do something for me.

HARRY   Right.

DENISE   You'd do something for me, wouldn't you?
           I promise it's nothing to do with the blindfold.

HARRY   That's good

DENISE   You might even enjoy it.

HARRY   What is it?

DENISE   No, that's not how it works.
           You have to say yes first.

HARRY   Yes first?

DENISE   And then I tell you what it is, otherwise it's no fun.

HARRY   Okay.

DENISE   Great!

HARRY   No, okay I understand, not okay I agree.
          I don't.

DENISE   That's a shame.

HARRY   Sorry

DENISE   Because I thought you wanted to make it up to me.

HARRY   I

DENISE   I thought you wanted to make it up to me so we can
          go on as friends, but if you're not bothered.

HARRY   No it's not that it's

DENISE   No, no, say no more.

HARRY   Alright.

DENISE   Alright?

HARRY   Deal.

DENISE   Shake on it?

          Blackout.

14.

DENISE *stands alone, waiting.*

DENISE   You alright in there?

HARRY   (*Offstage*.)
          Yes.

DENISE   Come out then.

HARRY   (*Offstage*.)
          No.
          I'm actually
          I'm actually just going to go home

DENISE   No you're not.

HARRY   (*Offstage*.)
          No, I am.
          I'm just going to go home now. Thanks but

DENISE   I've got your clothes here Harry.
          You'll have to go home in the nude.
          Like Woof!

HARRY   (*Offstage*.)
          Like who?

DENISE   Woof
          He was a boy who turned into a dog.

HARRY   (*Offstage*.)
          Ah-ha

DENISE   And then when he turned back he was in the nip.

HARRY   (*Offstage*.)
          Right.
          I don't think I
          Saw that

          I'm coming out now.

DENISE   Come on then

          HARRY *enters, in quite small shorts and a Lycra
          top.*

HARRY   I hate it.

DENISE   You look

HARRY   Don't you dare

DENISE   Great. You look great.
          Great.

HARRY   These are

          HARRY *pulls at the crotch of his shorts.*

DENISE   You'll be glad of them when you're doing star-
          jumps and your bits and pieces aren't flying
          everywhere.

HARRY   Oh my God

DENISE   I think you look
          Perfect.
          You've got excellent definition.

HARRY   Right, thank you thank you that's enough.

DENISE   You'll be beating them off with a stick.

HARRY   The wrinklies.

DENISE   They're not all that wrinkly some of them.

HARRY   No?

DENISE   Rose is still in her fifties.

HARRY   Oh, well that changes everything.

          DENISE *picks up her bag to get changed.*

DENISE   Me next, excuse me.

          DENISE *exits.* HARRY *half-shouts after her.*

HARRY   Why do they put mirrors in men's bathrooms?

DENISE   (*Offstage.*)
          What was that?

HARRY   I don't see the point of them.

DENISE   (*Offstage.*)
          Make-up.

HARRY   Eh?

DENISE   (*Offstage*.)
         They're for doing make-up!

HARRY   Men's ones though?

DENISE   (*Offstage*.)
         Don't be so narrow-minded!
         Hair then.

         HARRY *touches his thin hair.*

HARRY   Maybe.
         I stopped looking in them. When we married,
         I suppose. I was always well turned out, I hope
         anyway. But I wouldn't look at them. I'd just sort
         of look past them. She was forever flicking bits of
         hair back or down or bothering at it somehow. I'd
         watch her putting her face on for half an hour and
         I'd wonder how she could do it.

         All those little
         Disappointments.
         I'd rather not bother.
         I'd rather not know.

         So I didn't. For years. After, you know. You catch
         sight of yourself from time to time in a mirror at
         the shops or whatever. Rear-view mirror. But you
         don't really look. Not really. And then today, just
         then, I did.

         And you know what I said?

DENISE   (*Offstage*.)
         No?

HARRY   I said, you're an old man.
         You're an old, old man.
         In tiny shorts.

         *Lights! Music! Zumba! HARRY dances, tentatively
         at first, but then with increasing energy. After a time
         DENISE joins him. It is some excellent Zumba.*

         Blackout.

15.

HARRY *is on his phone, he has been angry for some time.*

HARRY   It's not that simple.
No. No listen

Well they'll just have to
I don't know
I don't know

I didn't say I don't care
Though actually.
Ah-ha. Yes.
Yes.
Well naturally
Yes, but

It makes all the difference, you'd be surprised
what a
Yes

No, that's not what I

DENISE enters. HARRY beckons her over.

DENISE   ?

HARRY   Ah, hold on
Let me just

More beckoning.

She's actually here with me now
Yes, Denise, yes
Here

Hands phone across.

DENISE   Hello there.
Thanks Mr Jones, hi.
Yes we got the letter, thank you.

I'm sure he did, yes
I'm sorry about that.

It's actually quite simple, we have a regular
attendee who has access issues and she's brought to

and from the class by her carer, who only actually
works until nine.
Is only permitted to work until nine, I should say
On her current contract, and so

Yes
And so any movement of the starting time of the
class would mean that she simply isn't able to attend
At all.
No well why would you
You never do ask.
Good

So we'll just leave it all…
As it is
For the moment, good.
Thank you, Mr Jones
Robert, fine
Thank you
Bye thank you bye.

Hands back the phone. HARRY *claps.*

HARRY   Bravo!
           Well played, well played!

DENISE   Thank you.

HARRY   You had him
           You had him over a barrel
           The bastard

           Sorry, but
           Great stuff.

DENISE   Thanks, Harry.

HARRY   Played them at their own game

DENISE   I meant it
           Sheila can't just have her hanging on.

HARRY   So we're just

DENISE   Back to normal.

HARRY   Great

DENISE   Just a load of silliness
          They hadn't thought

HARRY   That's just the thing.
          We've been meeting at five for
          Well for years
          They get used to consistency
          That's how you build up
          Consistency
          So if you

DENISE   Switch it around

HARRY   If you go –

DENISE   Switching it around

HARRY   Switching it around, yes
          If you go
          Switching it around it just won't
          You won't get anywhere
          So five it is and five it will stay

DENISE   What a team!

HARRY   Yes.

DENISE   What is it?

HARRY   Nothing.

DENISE   There was a thing just there, did you notice it?

HARRY   No? No thing.
          There was no thing. Nothing.

DENISE   You noticed it.

HARRY   It's nothing.
          Can we
          Can we move on.

DENISE   Move on?

HARRY   Yes, move on.

DENISE   You've gone all council.

HARRY   Well, I can turn it on too
           From time to time.

           Have you done
           Something, with your eh

DENISE   My hair?

HARRY   Yes, your hair

DENISE   I might of.

HARRY   I thought so.

DENISE   And?

HARRY   Sorry?

DENISE   You were halfway through a compliment there,
           Harry
           Don't stop now.

HARRY   It's pretty.

           You off somewhere nice after?

DENISE   Not especially.

           Are you staying?

HARRY   Hmm? No, no I'll be on my way tonight.
           It took me until Saturday afternoon to get my
           walk back.
           I was going around like John Wayne.

           Mimes a wide-stanced hobble.

DENISE   It's quite tough on the groin.

HARRY   Yes, well, I'll

DENISE   Groin isn't a rude word, Harry.

HARRY   No, well it is a

           I suppose not.

DENISE   Bit more energetic than council.

HARRY   Yes. Well. I don't know.

DENISE	Get pretty wild, does it?
HARRY	Best believe it.
DENISE	Wild?
HARRY	Can get very heated
DENISE	Tell me.
HARRY	Well...
DENISE	Have to fend them off with your hammer?
HARRY	Yes. Well, no, but
DENISE	Maybe I should come along?
HARRY	You come?
DENISE	Yes.
HARRY	To the
DENISE	Yes. You could do with some new blood I reckon.
HARRY	Right.
DENISE	Unless that's against regulations. You let women in don't you? You've let Rose in. Rose can't read.
HARRY	Rose can read.
DENISE	News to me. She's in The Lions.
HARRY	Possibly.
DENISE	Dirty bitch.
HARRY	I don't know about that.
DENISE	So what do you say? Fair's fair. I like things with you.
HARRY	So do I. I mean. With you.
DENISE	So it's a date?

HARRY   If you say so.

DENISE   I do.

          Blackout.

16.

HARRY *is closing the door to the hall.* DENISE *stands away from him.*

HARRY   (*To offstage.*)
          Safe home. Watch the ice.
          Right now, ta-ta.

          Closes the door.

          Alright?

DENISE   Yeah

HARRY   I mean it's not the Zumba but you can still
          Gets the heart going.

DENISE   Yeah

          HARRY *goes to the trestle table to take it down.*
          Waits for DENISE. *She stays where she is.*

HARRY   I'll get this away then.

DENISE   Right, yeah.

          HARRY *takes the table down himself, a little*
          awkwardly. DENISE *stays silent.*

          Is it always like that?

HARRY   Oh, more or less.
          Jack was being even more awkward than usual
          Throwing spanners in the works.
          But that's just his game, you know.
          Whatever keeps him happy.
          Did you have a good

Well, not a good, it's never a good time but
Well, thanks for coming.

DENISE   It's fine.

HARRY *has his bag with him, takes out a wrapped
           sandwich.*

HARRY   Ham and pease, you?

DENISE   I'm not hungry.

HARRY   You sure

DENISE   I'd just like to get on

HARRY   What's wrong?

DENISE   Nothing's wrong, Harry.

HARRY   I've upset you. They've upset you.
           Look, if it's Rose she's just

DENISE   It's not Rose.
           It's not anybody I just.

           It's not the council, is it?

HARRY   No, I never said it

DENISE   I just thought it was, I just thought it was the
           council.

HARRY   No, it's the Billingham Improvement Committee.

DENISE   And you're Chair

HARRY   That's right.

DENISE   And what do you do?

HARRY   I sort of, bang the, and I call it all to order.

DENISE   Not you, the committee.
           The Improvement Committee.
           What's it for?

HARRY   So it's not a council but

DENISE   No it's not a council.

HARRY   But it sort of does a lot of the jobs of a council.
            It's an Improvement Committee.

DENISE   And do you?

HARRY   Do we what?

DENISE   Improve things?

HARRY   Well we try
            You tell me.

DENISE   I haven't seen that many improvements recently.
            I didn't hear many improvements suggested

HARRY   Right.

DENISE   I just heard a lot of

HARRY   What? A lot of what?

DENISE   Just leave it, I shouldn't have spoke.
            I shouldn't have come.

HARRY   There's no need to be like that, have a sandwich,
            mine's

DENISE   I know what yours is, I'm not hungry.
            I asked you, what do you do
            What do you do that improves?
            What do you do that's an improvement?

HARRY   Well you wouldn't, not necessarily.
            We do little things.
            That the council won't necessarily
            Like, you know the monument in the square?
            With the drinking fountain?

DENISE   To be honest

HARRY   We did it up.

DENISE   That's great.

HARRY   Raised the money, did it up.

DENISE   That's really good.

HARRY   And the play park?

DENISE   By Woodlands?

HARRY   That's it.
         We cut the grass on that, there's a rota.

DENISE   So what was all that?

HARRY   What was all what?

DENISE   All that, in there?

HARRY   A normal meeting.

DENISE   Normal?

HARRY   As far as you get a normal one yes

DENISE   Well that's a shame.

HARRY   What's a shame?

DENISE   It's a shame you spend an hour every week with
         those fucking terrible people.
         Excuse the

HARRY   You're excused.

DENISE   They're
         Shits
         Harry. I don't know how you can't
         Right, so. Jack

HARRY   Difficult man

DENISE   Is he? He was the only one talking any sense as far
         as I can see.
         You're talking about this centre, this

HARRY   Gorse Grove.

DENISE   Gorse Grove, and it's what? It's a sort of outward-
         bounds thing, is it?
         For young people.

HARRY   Not exactly.

DENISE   Or for young offenders, young, at-risk, young
         People, right?

HARRY   Well, it's complicated.

DENISE   Complicated is fine, I can do complicated.
           I read the *Observer*, Harry.

HARRY   It's a secure, it's a supposedly secure
           Yes outward-bounds.

DENISE   Right.

HARRY   Billingham Borstal.

DENISE   Yeah, right, that's what you said

HARRY   Yes

DENISE   And it got a laugh, didn't it?
           Billingham, whatever.
           And you're all talking about it and I have a look at
           the proposal and I've actually read a bit about it,
           and I know a woman who's, who's in my book
           club, and who had a lot to do with getting the site
           secured and the grants, and the local authority, and
           the council, and has been joining all of that up.

HARRY   You alright?

DENISE   Sorry, yes, I'm, just let me
           So I know a bit about it, actually, even if I didn't say
           And you're talking about it and you're the
           Improvement, whatever
           And I've never heard, actually, I've never heard such
           Ignorance. So much, excuse me, so much utter
           shite being talked, Harry. Just so much small-
           minded, narrow shite.

HARRY   It's a borstal!

DENISE   I know, that was your joke and they laughed, but
           you're serious.

HARRY   I don't think there's anything wrong with trying to
           keep the people, the children, of this town safe from

DENISE   Go on.

HARRY   From a load of junior criminals, and there's plenty
           that agree with me.

DENISE   I can see that.

HARRY   I don't have anything against them.

DENISE   Of course you don't.

HARRY   None of us, not one, has anything against these
institutions.
But we're a small community, and community
matters and I don't know what good, what
improvement, if that's not a dirty word to you,
we'll get by having a load of thugs from down
south or wherever the hell they've come from
shooting up drugs a hundred yards from the
school gates.
Alright?
I don't want it.

DENISE   Not in your back yard.

HARRY   Not in. Right.
So that's what Jack started with, two weeks ago.
'Oh it's the worst kind of Nimby-ism.'
Nim-what-ism?
'Nimby-ism,' he says. 'Not In My Back Yard,
that's you.'
Well I don't want it in my back yard, actually. And
what's wrong with that?
Because it's nice round here!
Oh you can smirk but it is.
We've kept it nice
We've bothered. We've bothered with the gardens
and we've paid attention to all of that, and it's nice
and we don't want it spoiled.
We don't want it spoiled.
What's wrong with that?

DENISE   So where do they go, Harry? Where do they build
the thing?

HARRY   Any-bloody-where else!

DENISE   I don't want an argument.

HARRY   Well you've got one, you don't get to
Just decide when we're having one and when
we're not.

DENISE   Don't I?

HARRY   No! Not if you're calling it, all of this
          If it's just shite to you.
          I've put a lot into this community. For years.
          I've cut the verges, I've brought the Meals on
          The Meals on Wheels, who's been the wheels?
          I have.
          And I'm down the Citizens, learning forms,
          learning God knows what
          And just to try to help someone, somehow, because
          I think that's probably what she might have
          wanted, or
          I mean
          Who makes sure they don't turn the park into,
          a bloody, estate.
          Who stops them filling the hills with bloody wind
          farms?

DENISE   Oh you've buggered the wind farms as well,
          have you?

HARRY   Yes! I have!
          As a matter of fact.
          I have. We have.
          And we've done more. We've done
          Who looks after, and looks out for, for all of it, eh?
          I do. We do. The Billingham Improvement
          Committee do.
          So you can save your, bloody
          Condescension. Alright?

DENISE   Alright.

          You finished?

          Blackout.

17.

HARRY *is putting down the trestle table, alone and in a rush, he snaps his finger under one set of legs.*

HARRY   Bugger!

          Picks the table up and carries it rapidly to the wall, DENISE enters.

DENISE   Hullo.

HARRY   Hi.

DENISE   You erm
          You rushing off again.

HARRY   What, no

DENISE   No flowers this time?

HARRY   No, I just want to get going.
          Out of your hair.

DENISE   You're not in my hair.

HARRY   I've things to be seeing to.

DENISE   Wind farms to tear down?

HARRY   Firebombing an orphanage actually.

          Drowning some kittens.

DENISE   Right. Hunting hoodies.

HARRY   Exactly.
          Then I'm going to pop round the donkey sanctuary.
          Kneecap a few of the hairy bastards.

          DENISE *laughs.*

          I'm very sorry about my behaviour last week.

DENISE   You don't have to say that, I'm fine.

HARRY   I know you
          I know you are, you're always fine.
          You're very
          Good.
          I don't mean that as an insult.

DENISE   I didn't take it as one.
           Funny sort of insult.

HARRY   I did just want to know, though
           Why didn't you speak up?
           If you were so incensed?
           Say something.

DENISE   Because I'm not very good at it!
           I get
           I don't want to be shouted down by a room of
           red men.

HARRY   And Rose.

DENISE   And bloody Rose
           Sorry.

           I'm not good at it.
           But I'm getting better
           I hope.
           I hope I'm getting better at it.

HARRY   Well I didn't want you to think I was making small
           of any of what you said.
           It's hit home.

DENISE   Has it really?

HARRY   Some of it.

           I really do have to get off.

DENISE   You won't stay for

HARRY   No.

DENISE   No hard feelings.

HARRY   Great.
           Thanks.

           Night then.

DENISE   I had a look at that fountain

HARRY   Fountain?
           Oh the. Yes.

DENISE	You've done a nice job of it.
HARRY	Thank you.
DENISE	It is nice. Not just the fountain but It's all nice.
HARRY	I think so, yes.
DENISE	I never actually thought about verges much. I suppose I'd figured they just sort of looked after themselves. Or maybe the government.
HARRY	You thought the government cut the verges?
DENISE	I don't know, I'm not a verge expert.
HARRY	If only!

Pause.

DENISE	What are you doing on the 11th?
HARRY	On the 11th?
DENISE	Saturday week.
HARRY	Well that depends Usually I'd Well Gyffords possibly.
DENISE	The garden centre?
HARRY	It is a garden centre, yes. I need, well I'll usually be needing something for the garden.
DENISE	It's December. What do you need for the garden in December?
HARRY	Well, it I like the café.
DENISE	Right. It's a good café is it?
HARRY	Not particularly but It's alright and

DENISE   I can't imagine you with a spade somehow.

HARRY   No?

DENISE   Didn't think you'd be a big gardener.

HARRY   I'm not, I've never been into it really.
Claire was keen but

DENISE   Okay.
I've never known what her name was.

HARRY   Claire. She was called Claire.
She was a very
She liked a project, but she never really.
The garden was where most of them started.
Pond. Rockery. An arbour but actually she finished
the arbour.
But there were always so many bits and pieces that
she'd lost interest in, or got distracted.
She loved the garden.
We had a bit of bother with the strawberries,
getting pinched by crows and that. Tried putting
nets over them you know but they still went for
them and they just tore right through the nets.
So she decided to put up a sort of scarecrow.
Patched it together with a pair of my old cords and
a sweatshirt.
Just left it up all year round, whether it was
strawberry time or not.
And in the winter she'd go out and put a jacket and
a hat on it, to keep it warm you know, and then in
the summer she'd take them off again.

DENISE   She sounds fun.

HARRY   Oh she was fun.
I haven't had the heart to get rid of him, or
anything really.
But I've never bothered with the jacket so he looks
Well, like a sort of snapped umbrella.
Jiggered
My dad was a farmer / and he used to say

DENISE   Was he?

HARRY   'By the time I'm finished I will be finished.
         Jiggered, that's what I'll be.'

         Like a broken tool. Like a thing.
         That's what he looks like now.

         HARRY *starts laughing*.

DENISE   Don't see what's funny.

HARRY   He's just a bloody
         A bloody
         You know, a bloody, rag man.
         He looks
         Oh he looks.

         He stops laughing.

         He looks sad, actually.

         Pause.

DENISE   Would you like to come to a party?

HARRY   I
         No. No.

DENISE   Alright.

HARRY   No, I don't mean.
         But no, there's actually
         I've got to be somewhere.

DENISE   Gyffords café doesn't count.

HARRY   No no. It isn't
         As a matter of fact I can't go to Gyffords either
         Or your party.
         But thank you, it's very
         I mean, after
         It's very kind of you to ask.

         Blackout.

18.

There is a small Christmas tree on the table, HARRY *is packing away his papers.* DENISE *enters.*

DENISE   I am freezing my arse off!
          I'm going to buy a gillet.

HARRY   A what?

DENISE   A gillet.
          It's a sort of outside vest.
          No sleeves.

HARRY   Oh, like a jockey.

DENISE   No, I don't think so.

          Indicates the tree.

          That's nice.

HARRY   What? Oh

DENISE   That yours?

HARRY   It is I
          Was only five pounds.

DENISE   That's a

HARRY   Five forty-nine.

DENISE   Well

HARRY   I just thought it'd brighten things up a bit
          We're talking about the carol concert so, you know

DENISE   'Tis the season.

HARRY   That's right
          It is the season.

DENISE   Tenor

HARRY   What?

DENISE   You're a tenor, I reckon
          You look like a bass, but you're a tenor.

HARRY   Oh, no
          I won't be singing
          And we don't really bother
          I mean
          It's only really 'We Wish You A Merry Christmas'
          and that so we don't really bother dividing it all up.
          But I was actually, at school
          I have a surprisingly high voice
          Surprisingly

DENISE   Well not to me. I can smell a tenor.

HARRY   Right, yes.

DENISE   How was the meeting?

HARRY   Oh fine
          We decided to, well I decided to
          We're giving the money to charity
          The carol money you know.

DENISE   Are you?

HARRY   Usually it goes to the fire station, for their
          Well it actually bought them a new television for,
          you know
          For the rec room

DENISE   That's lovely

HARRY   Yes, it was actually
          But no, this year it's going to, erm
          Amnesty International

DENISE   That is a surprise.

HARRY   They do work abroad, mostly on human rights and
          all of that

DENISE   I know who Amnesty are, Harry

HARRY   There was a bit in the paper
          Jack brought it in

DENISE   Good old Jack

HARRY   Anyway, I thought you'd be pleased

DENISE   I am.

          I've got a bit of news too.

HARRY   Oh yes?

DENISE   I'm doing a book.

HARRY   Reading one?

DENISE   Writing.

          It was after what you said, actually.
          What you said about what you do at the Citizens
          whatsit.
          You said 'Some of the things they come to you
          with…'
          And I said 'It'd make a good book, that' and
          you said
          'Yes,' or something.
          Anyway, it got me thinking.
          'What would I write about?'

HARRY   I see.

          HARRY *takes a small wrapped package from his
          pocket and looks at it*. DENISE *doesn't see it*.

DENISE   'What's my book about?'
          Because everyone's got one in them, they say,
          don't they.
          So I'm thinking, wait for it
          I'm going to do the book group.

          Not my book group, mine's boring as shite but
          a fictional one.

HARRY   I see.

DENISE   Book about a book group.
          Wheels within wheels.

HARRY   Ah-ha.

DENISE   Backstabbing. Betrayals.
          Bit of hanky-panky.
          Like your Lions.
          Wife-swapping. Scandal.

Anyway, there's this one called Sandy
Like Sandy from *Grease*,
Maybe she was named after her or something
I don't know,
And she's the quiet one, and she never really
speaks up for herself.
And the rest of them
They just sort of ignore her?
And there's one in particular, who's the leader
I suppose and he went to university down south,
and he talks over her all the time.
Makes small of her.
Never really includes her ideas or suggestions.
But then she writes this book
She's been writing it in secret for years.
Just writing away, just her own little secret life.
And it comes out, and it's a huge success, and it's
on the Costa coffee awards and they're all dead
nice about it but secretly fuming
And then the bolshy southern type, he's the most
jealous of the lot of them.
So he bumps her off.
Pushes her in front of the 486 to Humberton.

So.
What do you think?

HARRY   I like it.

DENISE   Do you?

HARRY   I'd watch it.
           Probably
           I don't have
           Well I do have a telly but I barely
           But I'd watch that.

DENISE   It's a book, Harry.
           I'm talking about a book.

HARRY   Course you are.
           Sorry.

DENISE   Are you alright?

HARRY   I'm fine, just
           Tired.

           Yawns.

DENISE   I'm with you there.
           I had another bad night.

HARRY   Couldn't sleep?

DENISE   Insomnia.
           Actually no. Sciatica. I just say insomnia to make
           me sound young and mysterious.
           It's either sciatica or indigestion, anyway.

HARRY   Too much fancy food.

DENISE   Ha!

HARRY   Too much fine living.

DENISE   That must be it.

           Well you get off.

HARRY   I'm going.

           HARRY *collects his bag. He reaches for his*
           pocket. Thinks again.

           I think I will.

DENISE   Will what?

HARRY   I think I will come Saturday
           If it's still on the table
           I mean, if you don't mind.

DENISE   Of course I don't mind.
           You sure?

HARRY   Do me good to get out of the house.

DENISE   Good. Great!
           I'm glad. I'll text you the address.

HARRY   Oh no!

DENISE   You'll be fine. It's just past Bracknell Park.

HARRY   Oh right.

DENISE   I'll introduce you to Janine.

HARRY   She a friend of yours?

DENISE   Obviously.
You'll like her.

HARRY   Oh
Oh well I'm not looking for anything like that.

DENISE   Course not.
I'll introduce you anyway.

HARRY   Will eh [he]
Be there?

DENISE   Ken? Yes, Harry, Ken will be there.

HARRY   Lovely, that's
I've wanted to meet him.

DENISE   Course you have.

HARRY   Will I need to wear anything special?

DENISE   What were you thinking?

HARRY   I don't know, it's been a while since I've been to a party.

DENISE   Come as you are.
You're always smart anyway.

HARRY   Oh that's very.

DENISE   You dress like a sort of posh sort of farmer.

HARRY   Oh.
I suppose I'll take that as a compliment.

DENISE   Best you can expect.

HARRY   I'm sure.

DENISE   Saturday night then.

HARRY   Saturday night.

Blackout.

19.

HARRY *is sitting at the table.* DENISE *enters. She's wearing a necklace. She's carrying her phone in one hand.*

DENISE   Don't get up on my account!

HARRY   Hello!

DENISE   Still worn out I suppose?
            Tearing up the dance floor.

HARRY   Oh! No.
            Don't remind me.

DENISE   I thought Janine was going to sprout a hernia.

HARRY   I did have to have a good lie-down when I got home.

DENISE   Sleep it off!

            DENISE *puts her phone down on the table.*

HARRY   No, no! I was just
            I'm not as young as I used to be.
            I hope I didn't cause you any trouble.

DENISE   You were great.

HARRY   Actually, Denise, I have some news

DENISE   You can still move a bit, can't you?

HARRY   I had a lovely time

DENISE   So did I.

HARRY   Good. Good.
            What time did you get home?

DENISE   I couldn't tell you.

HARRY   You were a little shaky on your feet.

DENISE   Felt like a teenager, carrying my shoes in one hand.

HARRY   So did I!
            When I got home I had to sleep sitting up.
            Was all spinning round. I had to have an
            Alka-Seltzer.

DENISE   You old rogue.

HARRY   Aye.

DENISE   You and Janine seemed to be getting on?

HARRY   Oh. She's not so bad.

DENISE   She's great. Her husband left her a few years ago.

HARRY   She told me. For a / chiropodist

DENISE   Chiropodist.
I know, she's furious about it.
As if there's anything wrong with chiropody, I think she thinks it's dirty.
Feet and whatever. But it's well paid!

HARRY   She asked me to take her dancing, properly, you know.

DENISE   Go for it!
Will you?

HARRY   No.
I don't want to get involved.
She's nice.

DENISE   We're not here for ever. You've got to take a chance from time to time.
Sometimes you've got to see something you want and grab hold of it. Don't let it go.

HARRY   Maybe you're right.

DENISE   So you'll do it?

HARRY   Do what?

DENISE   Call Janine.

HARRY   Oh, no. No.
Sorry.

DENISE   Don't apologise to me, I just think it'd do you good.

HARRY   I'm getting on fine as I am.

DENISE   I know you are.
It's not a criticism.

HARRY   Pleased to meet Ken.

DENISE   Oh. Yeah.
           I'm glad you had a word.

HARRY   Yes, we got on fine.

DENISE   What were you talking about?

HARRY   Nothing. Just. Anything.
           Talked about his job a bit.
           Didn't realise he worked in town.

DENISE   Didn't I say?

HARRY   He told me all about it.

DENISE   Good.

HARRY   He's an interesting man.

DENISE   If you say so.

HARRY   He left early.

DENISE   Did he?
           Well, he has a lot on, a lot to get on with, you know.
           And he doesn't like that sort of thing.
           Parties, socialising, it's not his sort of scene.

HARRY   No, well, we've got that in common.

           Pause.

DENISE   This is lovely

HARRY   What is?

DENISE   The necklace. I meant what I said.
           It's lovely.

HARRY   Oh it's nothing.

DENISE   It's not nothing it's

           I'm off for my wee.

HARRY   No problem.

           DENISE *exits. The phone on the table vibrates.*

HARRY *picks it up, looks at the message.*

He puts it back down, stung.

Pause.

DENISE *re-enters.*

DENISE   That's the tank empty and raring to go.

HARRY   Okay.

DENISE   You sure you won't stay?
           Could get back into your shorts?

HARRY   No.

DENISE   Don't know what you're missing
           It's Latin week, you could show us your flamenco.

HARRY   No.

DENISE   I think you'd make an excellent señor

HARRY   I don't want to.

DENISE   Alright.
           Only pulling your leg.

           The phone vibrates again.

           DENISE *picks up the phone and reads the
           message,* HARRY *watches, intently.*

HARRY   Everything alright?

DENISE   Yeah.

HARRY   Texting?

DENISE   Very observant.

HARRY   I want to ask you something.

DENISE   Mmm-hmm.

HARRY   Can you just
           Stop

DENISE   I'm listening

HARRY   Can you

           Do you have to reply to him right away?

           Pause. DENISE *looks to* HARRY.

DENISE   Reply to who?

HARRY   To whoever.

DENISE   What are you saying?
           Tell me Harry.

HARRY   It's the same as mine.
           The
           It's the same one as mine.

DENISE   Did you look at my phone?

HARRY   It buzzed.

DENISE   So you thought you'd have a snoop?

HARRY   It just popped up.
           It's the same as mine.
           The phone.

DENISE   Fine.

HARRY   Fine?

DENISE   It doesn't matter.
           It's my business.

HARRY   Not going to explain it then.

DENISE   I don't see why I should.

           It's complicated.

           HARRY *goes to leave*.

HARRY   I'm sure it is.
           Very complicated, I'm sure.

DENISE   You're angry with me now?

HARRY   No wish to be involved, thank you.

DENISE   Listen, I don't know what you think's going on.

HARRY   I think that's patently clear
          What's going on, don't you?
          See you next week.

          HARRY *opens the door.*

DENISE   Harry!
          Why you being like this?

HARRY   It's none of mine.

DENISE   That's right it's not.

HARRY   Does he know?

DENISE   Of course he doesn't know.
          What makes you think there's anything to know?

HARRY   Who is he?

DENISE   I don't think that's any of your business.
          It's just David.

HARRY   David.
          Did I meet David?

DENISE   Possibly.

HARRY   So he was there? Does Ken know him?

DENISE   That's not your concern.

HARRY   I know it's not my concern.

DENISE   So you can climb right off that high horse before
          I knock you off it.

HARRY   I'm just a bit

DENISE   A bit?

HARRY   Disappointed.

DENISE   Right, disappointed.
          Disappointed in me?

HARRY   Maybe I am a bit, yes.

          You don't do this sort of thing.

DENISE   How could you possibly know what sort of thing
           I do.

           Do you know me, Harry?
           What are the sort of things that I do?
           You didn't even know I was married till you tried
           a booty call.

HARRY   What's a booty call?
           Oh, I can guess.
           I'm just

DENISE   Disappointed, you said.
           Disappointed that I might be fucking someone
           behind his back and it's not you.

HARRY   That's ridiculous.

DENISE   Is it? I'm not sure it is.
           What's this about? What's any of this about?
           What's this about then?
           (*Grabs the necklace*.)
           Buy a lot of these for your friends do you?
           You don't strike me as the gift-giving type, usually,
           Harry.

HARRY   Don't I?

DENISE   No, you don't.

HARRY   I don't know where you've got this from
           Any of it
           You're not
           You're not turning it round on me.

DENISE   There's nothing to turn round!

HARRY   I don't agree with this sort of thing.
           Lions.
           This new

DENISE   This new what? There's nothing new about it.
           And you agree with it well enough when it suits you.
           You don't get to choose for me.
           What's fine with you isn't fine with some other man.

HARRY   I didn't say that, I didn't say any of that.
          It's you that's saying that.
          I like this, I like you.
          Just seeing you here, and I didn't mind
          Or I did but I didn't, not when I met him and got
          used to it.
          And I didn't mean anything, and I wasn't going to
          do anything.

DENISE   Weren't you? I don't believe you.

HARRY   And you've spoiled it.

DENISE   Spoiled.

          Pause.

          Had you noticed?
          I mean, is that why you thought

HARRY   What?

DENISE   Because you're not the only one who has, he has,
          I think

HARRY   Noticed?

DENISE   That I'm
          I'm not happy, Harry.
          I haven't been for a good while.

          But I'm not finished quite yet.

          And you

HARRY   There's nothing wrong with me
          I'm fine.

DENISE   No you're not, love.
          This isn't fine.

          I'm not fucking David.
          I'm just
          I'm not sleeping with him

          Maybe, in a few months
          Maybe
          Maybe not

But you don't get to have an opinion on that, do
you understand?
I'm not seeking your approval.
I'm not

I'm not her, Harry.
I'm not her.
I'm not and I don't want to be.

HARRY   I know that.

DENISE   And Ken
He's decent but

When he looks at me, it's like there's someone
creeping up from behind me, over my shoulder.
I wondered what it was, at first.
I thought his eyes might be going a bit, or his mind.
But I don't think they are.

And I get out of bed in the morning and I used to
feel his eyes on me
Across my body, thighs and whatever.
Now it's like
He's just trying not to look
Like it would be unkind to look?
Like he's doing me a kindness.

So David
I suppose I feel
I don't know.
I don't know yet.
Alright?

HARRY   Right.

DENISE   So I think
I think I need you to leave.

HARRY   No, that's

DENISE   No, I definitely do.
I do need you to leave, Harry.

HARRY   I just

DENISE	Please leave. They'll be here any minute.
HARRY	They'll be late They're always late.
DENISE	Not today. You need to go
	You need to go.
	Blackout.

20.

HARRY *is sat at the table, weighing his gavel in his hand.*

DENISE *enters.* HARRY *is in another world.*

DENISE	No flowers?
HARRY	Oh Sorry, I was
DENISE	I thought there'd at least be flowers. I was expecting a bouquet I'd brought a vase and everything.
HARRY	No, sorry I should
DENISE	Definitely you should
HARRY	Sorry, I
DENISE	You want to get yourself down to Gyffords.
	HARRY *smiles.*
HARRY	I thought you hated flowers.
	DENISE *smiles.*
	I'm heading off.
DENISE	Alright.

HARRY   But I wanted to
         Well

DENISE   You don't have to.

HARRY   No, it's not that
         I mean, I've
         I've got a bit of news.

DENISE   Oh?

HARRY   I'm giving it up, I've decided, I'm
         Well I'm stepping down from the committee.

DENISE   Right.

HARRY   Run its course I reckon.
         I've done my bit.

DENISE   Right.

HARRY   I thought you'd be
         Well, I thought it was for the best.

DENISE   I'm glad.

HARRY   Are you?

DENISE   I am
         I think it's the right thing to do.

HARRY   Reckon I'll just
         Push on with something else.

DENISE   You could get those bees!

HARRY   Yes, I could do that, yes.

         No.
         No, I don't think.

         Not bees I don't think, but.
         Something new.

DENISE   Just as well.
         I find beekeepers very monotonous.

HARRY   Right! Yes
         Probably.

So, anyway.
I won't be around all that often.
I'm sure I'll see you but

I won't be here next week.

DENISE   I'm sorry to hear that.
          Genuinely.

HARRY   I wanted to just / say

DENISE   No.

          Don't.

          Just take care of yourself, alright?

HARRY   Alright then.

          B'bye.

          HARRY *goes to leave*.

DENISE   Harry, hang on a sec.

HARRY   Yes?

          DENISE *stands by one end of the trestle table*.

          Oh
          Of course.

          HARRY *walks to the table, and he and* DENISE
          release the clips with perfect synchronicity.

          Blackout.

21.

A garden on a morning in early spring. A March light like blue zinc, and crows squawking in the distance.

The remains of a scarecrow, barely a few rough sticks pinned together, stands in the centre of a strawberry patch.

DENISE *enters, carrying a plastic bag.*

She takes out the coat she was wearing the first time they met, and hangs it on the scarecrow. She takes out a hat and a scarf too, and adds them.

She takes a step back to look at it.

Hold for a moment.

Blackout.

Other Titles in this Series

A Nick Hern Book

Trestle first published in Great Britain in 2017 as a paperback original by Nick Hern Books Limited, The Glasshouse, 49a Goldhawk Road, London W12 8QP, in association with Papatango Theatre Company and Southwark Playhouse, London

Cover image: Rebecca Pitt

Designed and typeset by Nick Hern Books, London
Printed in Great Britain by Mimeo Ltd, Huntingdon, Cambridgeshire PE29 6XX

A CIP catalogue record for this book is available from the British Library

ISBN 978 1 84842 701 3

www.nickhernbooks.co.uk

facebook.com/nickhernbooks

twitter.com/nickhernbooks